Contents

Chapter 1
What is the Web?

Getting Started

In this lesson you are going to connect your computer to the Internet. What is the Internet? It's a huge number of computers connected together, all over the world. Just as a few computers can be connected to form a network, so the Internet is an international network of networks.

In this book you will learn how to:

 Look up information on the Internet;

 Download pictures, text or software;

 Send and receive e-mail;

 Send large files such as scanned photographs without tying up the phone line for hours!

The program you use to look at the Internet is called a **Browser** and one of the most popular browsers is **Microsoft Internet Explorer**. To load it:

 Double-click on the icon for **Internet Explorer**.

 Or click **Start** at bottom left of the screen, then click **Programs**, then click

Internet Explorer

 You may see a dialogue box asking you if you wish to connect. If so, click **Connect**. An Internet page will appear on your screen – probably one that either your school or the manufacturer of your computer has set as a **default**.

You can go to a different page by typing a new **address**.

 Click in the **Address** box at the top of the window – the text will be highlighted.

Click here   *Figure 1.1: The Address box*   Go Button

 Type in **www.bbc.co.uk** and click on **Go**.

Now your screen should look something like the one below. It probably won't look quite the same because most people and companies are constantly updating their Web sites.

Address box   Menu bar   Toolbar

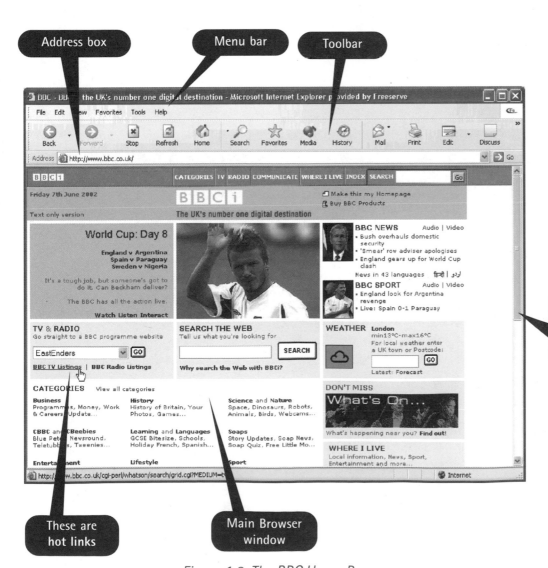

These are
hot links

Main Browser
window

Figure 1.2: The BBC Home Page

Note: How your screen looks will depend on how **Internet Explorer** has been set up.

You can scroll down to see the whole page

The **Media** button is not in Internet Explorer 5 but don't worry!

Note:

The rest of the Internet consists of files that are accessed in various ways.

The World Wide Web

The part of the Internet you are looking at here is the **World Wide Web** and this is a **Web page** on a **Web site**. Most large companies and organisations have a Web site and so do many individuals. There are hundreds of millions of Web pages stored on computers all over the world which you can access from your computer.

The first page on a site is known as the **home page** and this is the home page for the BBC.

Moving about the web

Web pages often have **hot links** (also called **hypertext** links). When you move the mouse pointer over a hot link, the cursor changes shape from an arrow to a hand.

 Try this now.

When you click on a hot area, the browser jumps to a new page.

 In the list of items down the left side, click on **Science** and see what comes up.

Hot links are marked by coloured text (usually underlined) or a graphic.

Click on the dinosaurs hot link (if there is one)

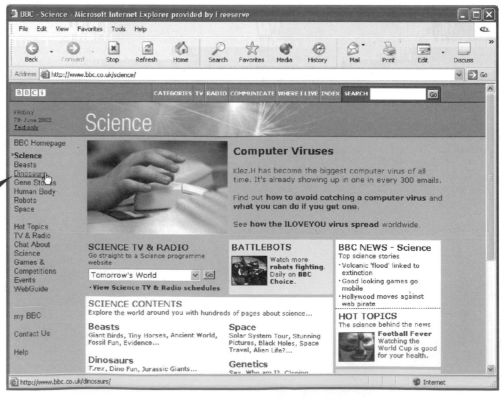

Figure 1.3: The BBC Science page

Click on **Dinosaurs** (or type in the address shown below if it isn't there).

You're now in a dinosaur world!

Figure 1.4: Walking with dinosaurs

Going back to a previous page

To go back to the previous page:

 Click on the **Back** button at the left of the toolbar. —————————— ⇦ Back

 Now click **Back** repeatedly to return to where you started.

 Click the **Forward** button to go forward to a previous screen. —————————— Forward

Note:

Favorites is spelt the American way in Internet Explorer!

Tip:

Be sure to select Favorites from the Menu bar, not the Tool bar (see Figure 1.1).

Adding a page to the Favorites list

To keep a note of a page so that you can return to it another time without having to remember and type the whole address, you can add it to a list of your favourite Web sites.

▶ Go back to the BBC home page.

▶ From the Menu bar choose **Favorites**, **Add to Favorites** and click **OK**.

Moving around the Internet

So far you've changed pages by:

▶ entering an address

▶ clicking on a link

▶ using the **Back** and **Forward** buttons.

We'll look at addresses in more detail. Typing a Web address is an easy way of getting quickly to the page you want. You will often see advertisements giving Web page addresses.

HOLIDAY.COM

Entering an address

Every Web page has a unique address. A typical Web site address is:

http://www.bbc.co.uk

All Web addresses start with **http://**. You don't have to type this in – it will be added automatically for you when you press the **Go** button.

When you click on a hot link, you go to a different page. Every single Web page has its own unique address, so the new address will have some extra bits on the end:

Figure 1.5: Web page address

www means world wide web.

bbc.co.uk is the **domain name**, showing the organisation that owns the site.

.co.uk shows that this is a company in the UK. International companies have domain names ending in **.com**.

Some other codes are **gov** for government, **org** for organisation, **ac** (**edu** in USA) for a college or university, or **sch** for a school.

Web sites belonging to different countries end in a two-letter country code – **uk** for the UK, **fr** for France, **de** for Germany, **es** for Spain, and so on.

Addresses *must* be typed in correctly, with no spaces and using small letters only except where shown.

Note:

You say this address out loud as "www dot bbc dot co dot uk" (leaving out the http:// and saying DOT for the full stops!)

Swot's Tip:

An address is also known as a **Uniform Resource Locator** or URL. **http** stands for HyperText Transfer Protocol, which is a set of rules used to make sure the data is correctly sent and received between the various computers on the Internet.

Why **de** for Germany and **es** for Spain?

Note:

It is common to leave out the http:// when giving a web site name although it is part of the address

Who do you think these web addresses belong to?

www.hazelwood.belfast.ni.sch.uk
www.disney.com
www.nasa.gov
www.payne–gallway.co.uk

 Click in the Address box, type in a new address: **www.howstuffworks.com** and press **Go**.

Scroll down to see the whole page

Figure 1.6: Another useful Web page

This is a site where you can find out how anything works, from your body to cars to computers and more.

Task: Choose something and find out how it works!

 Add the site to **Favorites** to make it easy to find again later.

Tip:

Favorites menu, Add to Favorites
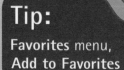

Returning to a 'Favorite' page

Suppose you decide you would like to go back to the BBC home page whose address you saved in **Favorites** earlier.

 Click the **Favorites** button on the toolbar.

 A list of pages that you have previously bookmarked appears on the left of your screen. Click **BBC Online HomePage**.

> Click it again to hide the list

The Links bar

Instead of adding a site to **Favorites** you can have it in view on the **Links bar**, under the Address bar. To do this you choose **Links** in the **Add to Favorites** window.

Figure 1.7: The Links bar

Tip:

The **Links** bar appears either at the right end of the Address bar or below it. If you don't see it, right-click the toolbar and select **Links**.

You can drag the addresses to rearrange them, or even drag a new one off the Address bar!

Ending an Internet session

When you have finished your Internet session, you should disconnect so that you are no longer using a phone line. There are several ways of doing this.

Note that closing Internet Explorer does not automatically disconnect you – you have to instruct the computer to disconnect.

While you are connected, this **Dial-up** icon appears in the bar at the bottom right of your screen.

 Right-click the **Dial-up** icon and select **Disconnect**. This disconnects the phone line, but does not close **Internet Explorer**.

 Close **Internet Explorer** by clicking the **Close** icon (X) at the top right of your screen, or by selecting **File, Close** from the menu bar.

Or, close Internet Explorer first...

An alternative way to finish an Internet session is to close **Internet Explorer** first, and then disconnect.

Click here

 Close **Internet Explorer** by clicking the **Close** icon (X) at the top right of your screen, or by selecting **File, Close** from the menu bar.

 You will see a message on your screen:

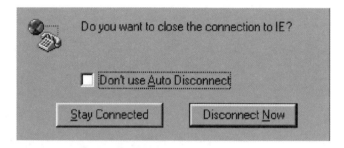

Figure 1.8: Disconnecting

 Click **Disconnect Now** to disconnect.

Pop-up advertisements

On some sites, you may find you are bombarded with unwanted 'banner' windows suddenly opening on their own. If this happens, close them at once and be careful not to click on any link or hotspot.

Chapter 2
Browsing

As you can see, it's easy to spend hours browsing the web, jumping from page to page. To look up a particular topic you can go to a reference site that will point you in the right direction. RefDesk is a good site to try.

▶ Load **Internet Explorer** by double-clicking the icon. ─────────

▶ Click in the Address box to select the current address.

▶ Type **www.refdesk.com** and press **Go**.

It's impossible to avoid all distractions!

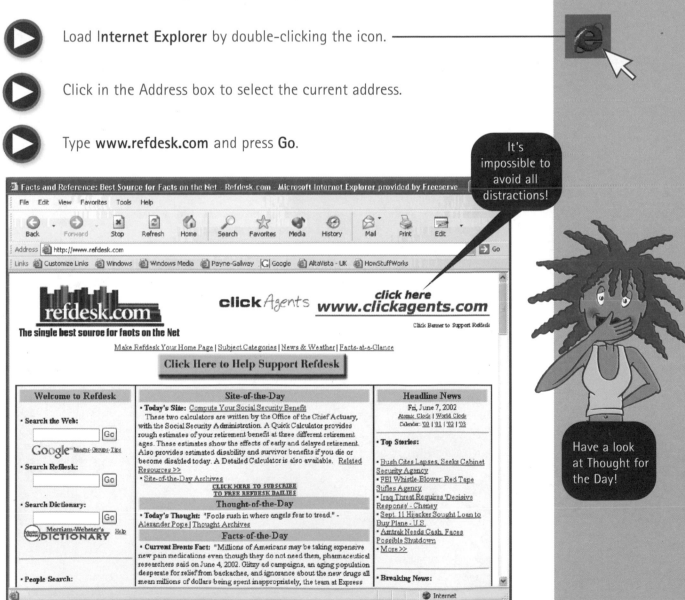

Figure 2.1: Refdesk, a useful reference site

Have a look at Thought for the Day!

Reference sites like this will have some facts themselves and also links to other sites.

Scroll down to the **Facts Search Desk** box.

You can look up several things in this box.

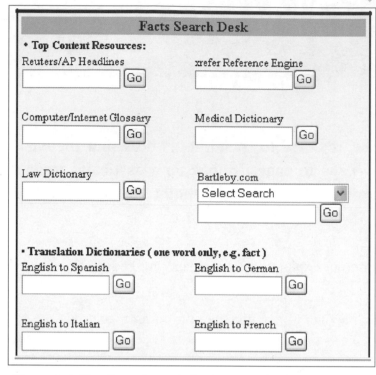

Figure 2.2: The Facts Search Desk on the RefDesk Web site

Using a dictionary

Do you know what **Campanology** means?

 Type it in the **Xrefer** box and click on **Go**.

This tells you where the word comes from and how to pronounce it as well as the meaning.

You can also look up words in other languages.

 In the **Translation Dictionaries**, have a look at the word for **Street** in French, German, Italian and Spanish.

 Go back to the **RefDesk** home page.

Using an encyclopedia

Suppose you are doing a project on the Ancient Romans. Bartleby is a good reference to look up information.

 Under **Bartleby.com** in the **Select Search** box, choose **Columbia Encyclopedia**, type **Ancient Rome** in the box below and click **Go**.

This shows a page full of links each with a short description of the article.

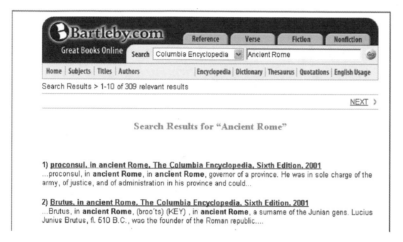

Figure 2.3: Looking up Ancient Rome

Tip:
You may have to scroll down a bit to find something good

This has found far too much – you probably only want to know about daily life.

 Scroll to the top of the **Bartleby** screen

 Type **Life in Ancient Rome** in the search box and click on **Go**.

This should be much more successful.

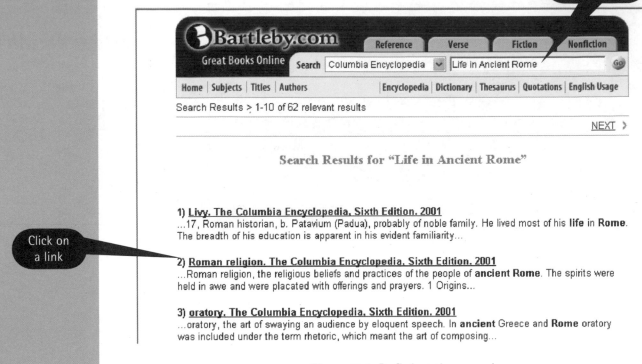

Click on a link

Figure 2.4: Refining the search

Try looking at some links. You can try different searches like **Gladiator**, **Colosseum** or **Pompeii** and see what comes up.

If the page is full of text and you can't find where something is mentioned, choose **Find (on this page)** from the **Edit** menu, type in the word and click **Find Next**.

You can now go back to the RefDesk site.

⬅
Back

▶ Click the **Back** button repeatedly until you are there.

▶ Add this page to **Favorites** for later.

Tip:
Favorites menu, Add to Favorites

Finding things out by Directories

Many sites have links arranged by subject matter, sometimes called **Categories**, so you can browse as in a library.

▶ Type **www.looksmart.co.uk** and click **Go**.

▶ Add the address to **Favorites** so you can return to it later.

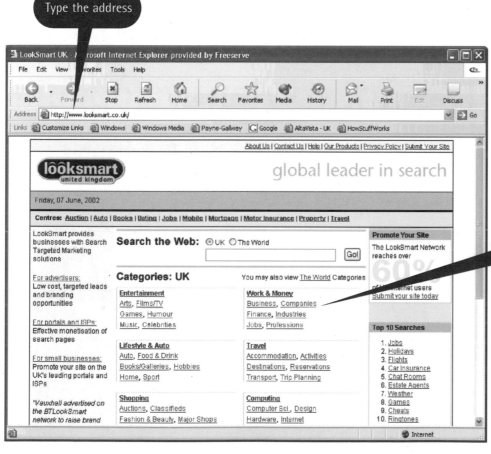

Figure 2.5: The LookSmart directory

LookSmart has a list of main **directories** each of which when clicked opens a list of subdirectories, and so on.

▶ For example, if you wanted to find out about museums to do with science and technology, scroll down to the **Library** section and click on **Arts & Humanities**, then **Museums & Heritage**, then **Science Museums**. (See Figure 2.6.)

Can you find the **Ironbridge Gorge Museum**?

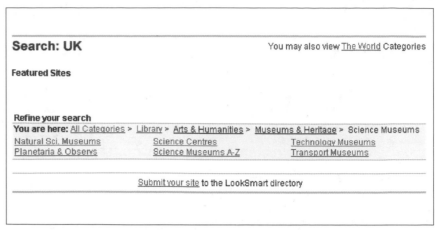

Figure 2.6: Searching through subdirectories

Tip:
Try Travel, Activities

Task: What can you find out about **Giants Causeway**?

The Encarta encyclopedia

Encarta Concise Encyclopedia is a good source of information. Although it has fewer articles than the De Luxe version which you have to pay for, there's still plenty there.

Note:
No **www** here

 Enter the address **encarta.msn.com/reference** and press **Go**.

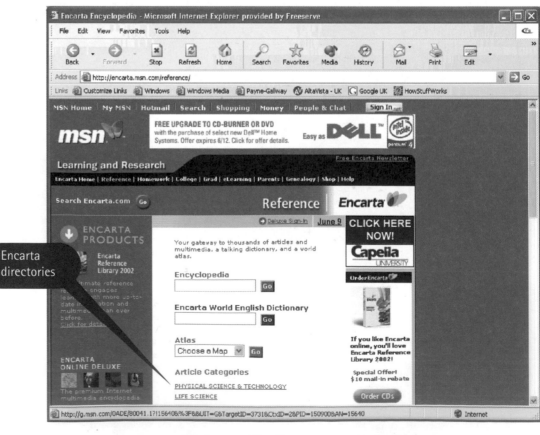

Be sure to add this page to **Favorites**

Figure 2.7: The *Encarta* encyclopedia

 Click on **Physical Science & Technology**.

 Click on **Astronomy & Space Science**.

| Mathematics |
| Physics |
| Chemistry |
| Earth Science |
| Paleontology |
| Astronomy & Space Science |
| Time, Weights, & Measures |
| Transportation |
| Communications |
| Computer Science & Electronics |
| Machines & Tools |
| Construction & Engineering |
| Industry, Mining, & Fuels |
| Military Technology |
| People in Physical Science |

Figure 2.8: Categories in an Encarta directory

Task: Find out the answers to the following questions:

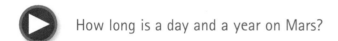 How long is a day and a year on Mars?

 How many moons does Mars have?

A quick way to enter an address

We'll now go back to the Encarta Reference page. Instead of using the **Back** button, here's another way.

 Start typing the address **http://encarta.msn.com/reference**

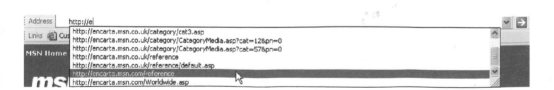

Figure 2.9: Selecting an address from a list

 Select the address in the list.

Tip:

As soon as you type **e**, a list will appear below as **Internet Explorer** recognises similar addresses

Maps on the Internet

You can look at a map of any country from here.

Task: In the **Atlas** box, choose the map of **Africa**.

Figure 2.10: Choosing a map

Task:

Find a detailed map of **Uganda**. What is the capital city? What lakes and mountains does it have? What countries does it share a border with?

Hint:

Uganda is in East Africa. Click on **East Africa** and find **Uganda**.

Make your own UK map

Going somewhere but don't have a map? You can use the LookSmart directory, which you bookmarked earlier.

▶ Click the **Favorites** button on the toolbar.

▶ Select **LookSmart** from the list on the left of the screen.

▶ In the **LookSmart** directories find **Reference Desk, Maps, UK Maps**.

▶ Click on **Multimap.com** and add it to **Favorites**.

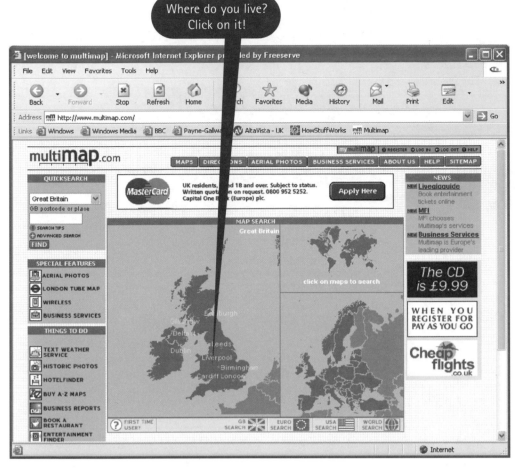

Figure 2.11: Getting a map

This site will draw you a map at different scales of almost anywhere in the world, with Europe and the USA in detail.

 Move the mouse over the UK outline and click on your home area. I've chosen East Anglia.

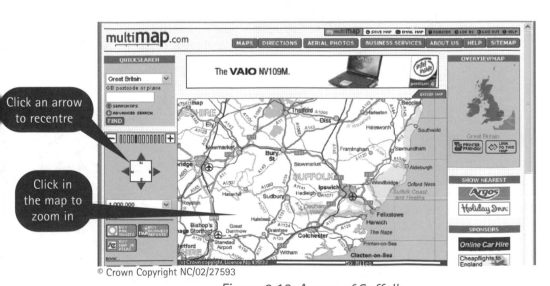

© Crown Copyright NC/02/27593

Figure 2.12: A map of Suffolk

Click the arrows to centre the map and click on the map to zoom in.

 Change the map scale as in Figure 2-12 and click on a town.

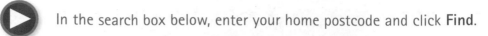 In the search box below, enter your home postcode and click **Find**.

Type your postcode here

Figure 2.13: Finding an area by postcode

You should have a streetmap of your area with a red circle round – or very near – your home! Click the Print button for a hard copy.

Ordnance Survey copyright allows you one copy for personal use

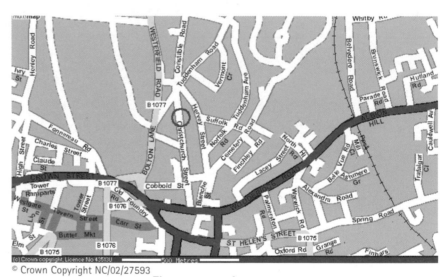

© Crown Copyright NC/02/27593

Figure 2.14: A street map

This is also most useful when visiting friends who give rather muddled directions!

"... then second left after the ice cream van, no right..."

Chapter 3
Search Engines

How deep is Loch Ness?

Where do okapis live?

Supposing you want to know the answer to a specific question. Some reference sites have a Search box to find something on that site, but to search the entire Internet we need something more powerful – a search engine!

Using a search engine

AltaVista is one of the most popular and easy-to-use search engines.

 Enter the address **www.altavista.co.uk**

Keyword searching

Directories

Figure 3.1: The AltaVista Search Engine

Note:
Sometimes a Web site switches to an alternative address

The page may not look quite like this – everything on the Internet changes regularly!

This is the UK branch of the US **AltaVista.com**.

Search engines usually have directories, news, local events and information but you can also search by entering a **keyword**.

Searching by keyword

AltaVista allows you type a word or phrase, and it then comes back with a list of related web pages. Let's find out about the Ancient Egyptians.

 Click **The Worldwide Web** button (see figure 3.1) to search worldwide.

 In the **Find this**: box enter the keywords **ancient Egyptians** and click **Search**.

Many references found!

AltaVista results for "ancient Egyptians"   87155 pages found.

Daily Bible Study - The **Ancient Egyptians**
Ancient Egypt. **Egyptians**. Discover the amazing truth of the Gospel. Eternal life. ... The **Ancient Egyptians**
Many are familiar with the old Egyptian empire solely because of the Israelite Exodus which ...
http://www.execulink.com/~wblank/egyptans.htm
More Pages From This Site

Ancient Egypt and the **Ancient Egyptians**. Pyramids, Pharaohs, Sphinx, Temples, Tombs, etc.
Dedicated to **Ancient** Egypt and the **Ancient Egyptians** - including free
articles,wallpapers,music,screensavers etc.
http://www.ancientnile.co.uk/
More Pages From This Site

Figure 3.2: Searching for references to Ancient Egyptians

Some pages may have nothing to do with ancient or even modern Egypt! This is because a lot of them contain 'ancient' or 'Egyptians' but not 'Ancient Egyptians', so we need to enter these as a phrase.

 Change the keywords to "**Ancient Egyptians**" and click **Search**.

This time there are far fewer pages found.

Tip:
Putting 'Ancient' with capital A will ignore 'ancient'

 Use double quotes

Figure 3.3: Refining the search

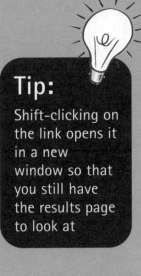

 Have a look at some of the references by clicking on the links.

The results are shown, 10 to a page, with (usually) the most relevant first. Scroll down to see subsequent pages.

Result Pages: 1 2 3 4 5 6 7 8 9 10 [next >>]

There may be some articles on Ancient Egypt that are being missed.

 Change the keywords to "**Ancient Egypt**" and click on **Search**.

This time, there are more pages found and the results look more varied, although with some unexpected items.

Figure 3.4: Results of a search

 Click on a link to see further information.

 Can you find the screen pictured in Figure 3.5?

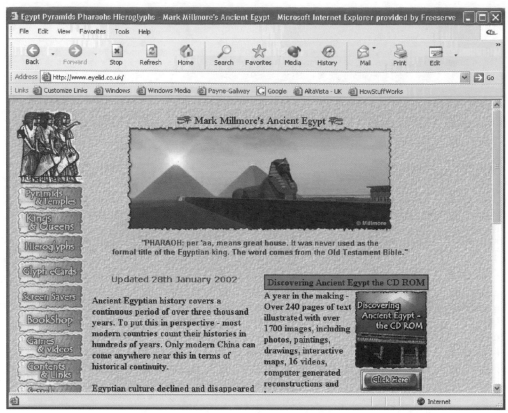

Figure 3.5: Ancient Egypt

Task: Go back to the **AltaVista** home page and try a new search.
Find the answers to the following question:

 What and where are the world's five longest rivers?

Missing page

You may find that your browser cannot find a page although you clicked on a link to it, and it displays something like this.

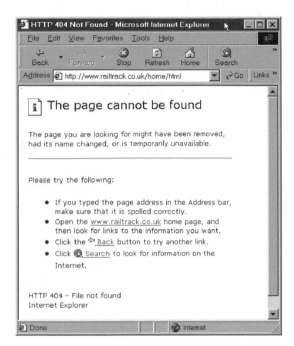

Figure 3.6: A missing page

Tip:
You'll see a similar message if you type an address in wrongly and the browser can't find it

Don't worry, this often happens! The Internet is growing so fast that many web pages have mistakes in their link addresses. This may be because the page that a link points to has been removed or had its address changed.

Including and excluding pages

Sometimes if the keyword you enter has other meanings or is a common name, **AltaVista** will return links to Web sites you are not interested in. Suppose you want to know about the planet Mercury. First we'll go back to the home page.

 Click on the down arrow on the **Address** box and a list comes down of all the addresses that have been typed in.

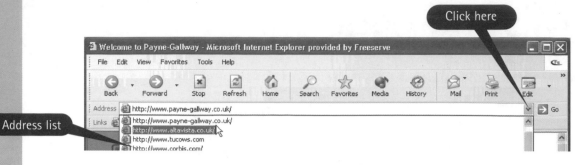

Click here

Address list

Figure 3.7: Choosing an address to go to

 Click on **http://www.altavista.co.uk** in the list.

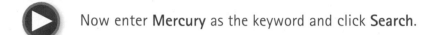 Now enter **Mercury** as the keyword and click **Search**.

Figure 3.8: Enter the keyword Mercury

The results come back.

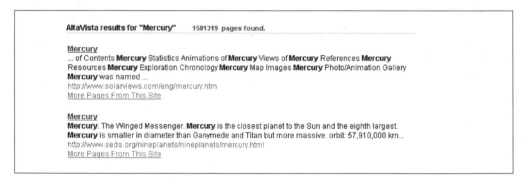

Figure 3.9: Search results

AltaVista didn't know whether you meant the planet, the metal element, magazines, outboard motors or a company name, and may also have found some references in other languages. You need to tell it to restrict the search.

If you put a plus sign (+) in front of a keyword, with no space, all pages containing this word will be listed. Similarly, putting a minus sign (−) in front will reject pages with this word.

You need to get references in English about planets and with no mention of metal, magazines or other distractions!

Type in keywords like those shown in Figure 3.10.

Figure 3.10: Entering a search to exclude unwanted references

This should bring back mostly pages on planets but anyone calling their personal Web site **Planet Mercury** will also appear!

Figure 3.11: References to the planet Mercury

Task:

Try searching for the following:

Polar bear
Python (the snake)
Tower of London
Leonardo (da Vinci)

 Close **Internet Explorer** and disconnect from the Internet.

Note:
You'll find how to do a more detailed search by clicking the **Advanced Search** link

Note:
A search engine has a 'Crawler' or 'Spider' program that runs all over the web building up an index of keywords. These may not always be relevant to what you're looking for, whereas the information in directories is compiled by hand and is always relevant.

Ready to look at another search engine? Try **www.google.com**

27

Chapter 4
Working Offline

You can do a lot of work without even logging on to the Internet, using pages that you have visited on previous occasions. This avoids tying up the phone line and cuts down on the phone bills!

▶ Open **Internet Explorer** either by double-clicking the icon or choosing **Start, Programs, Internet Explorer**.

▶ You may see a dialogue box similar to the one below. If so, click **Work Offline**.

Note:
If you are on a school network, you'll be on-line all the time.

Figure 4.1: Choosing to work offline

If **Connect Automatically** has been checked in this dialogue box, it will not appear next time and you will be automatically connected.

In that case, right-click the **Dial-up** icon in the bar at the bottom right of your screen and select **Disconnect**.

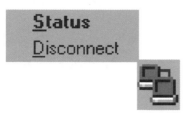

You are now working offline.

Tip:
Selecting File, **Work Offline** from the menu will not automatically disconnect you!

The Favorites List

The **Favorites** list is very useful when you are working on a project. You will often find you need to go back to pages you have visited previously. Sometimes you will want to delete items from the **Favorites** list or reorganise it so that the most used sites are near the top of the list.

 In **Internet Explorer**, click **Favorites** on the toolbar. Notice the **Favorites** list opens on the left.

Favorites

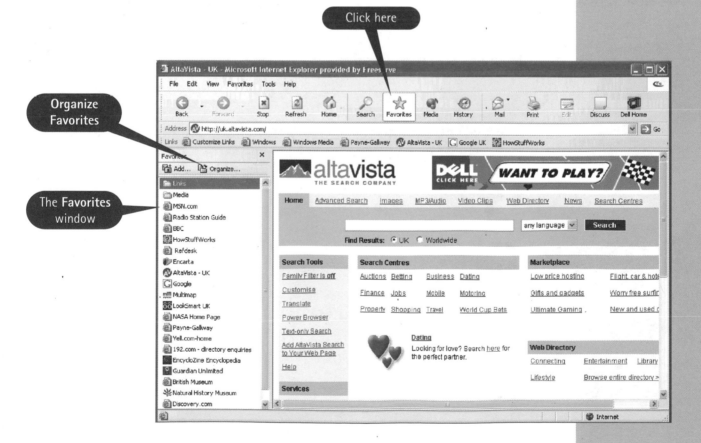

Figure 4.2: The Favorites list

You can ignore the yellow folders at the top, which may include **My Documents** which is where Windows puts your **Word** files. You can now choose a web page from the list.

Organising the Favorites list

The entries in the **Favorites** list appear in the order that they were added. You may want to change the order, perhaps moving the most useful ones up to the top.

Click on **Organize Favorites** (see Figure 4.2).

Tip:
You can select **Organize Favorites** from the **Favorites** menu

You can also group entries in other folders – see the **Help** menu

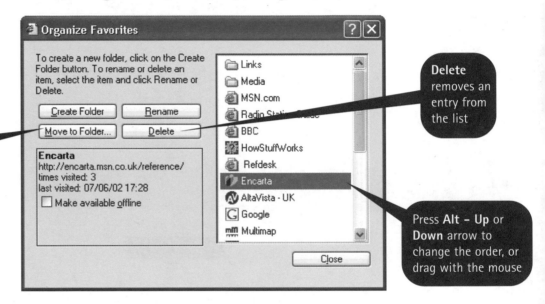

Delete removes an entry from the list

Press **Alt – Up** or **Down** arrow to change the order, or drag with the mouse

Figure 4.3: The *Organize Favorites window*

The **Organize Favorites** window lets you move entries around. For example, to move **Encarta** up:

 Select **Encarta** in the list.

 Hold down the **Alt** key and press the **Up** arrow.

Similarly, you can move items down, rename or delete them.

 Click the **Close** button.

You can hide the **Favorites** window by clicking the **Favorites** button on the toolbar to deselect it.

Note:
Deselecting is the opposite of selecting

The History list

Internet Explorer keeps track of all the pages you have visited and when. This is kept in the **History** list.

▶ Click on the **History** icon in the toolbar and notice the **History** list opens on the left.

▶ Click the arrow next to **View** and select **By Date**.

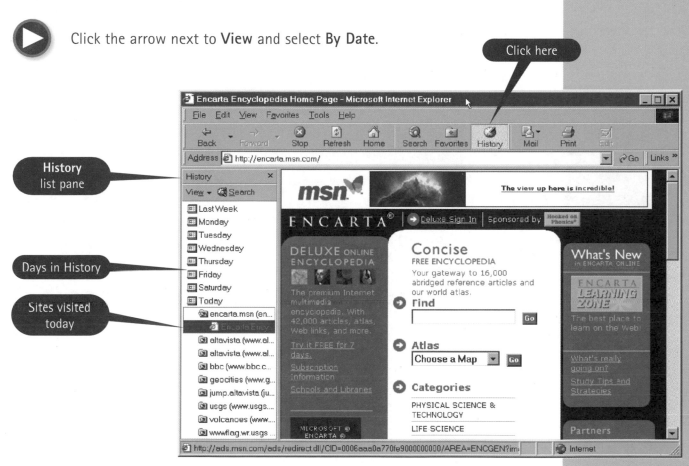

Figure 4.4: The History list pane

The **History** pane needs to be wider.

▶ Place the cursor over the right border until it changes to a double arrow.

▶ Drag it halfway across the window.

Tip:
A pane is a section of a window!

In the list, the pages visited are grouped by day, ending in **Today**. Clicking on an icon expands or contracts it.

▶ Click on the icon for **Today** to expand it, if it isn't already expanded.

Sites you've just visited

Click here to see the pages

How far back your History goes depends on how your browser is set up. This one is 2 weeks

Figure 4.5: The History list

A recent site you visited was **www.altavista.co.uk**.

▶ Click on the name.

The list now shows all the pages visited on that site.

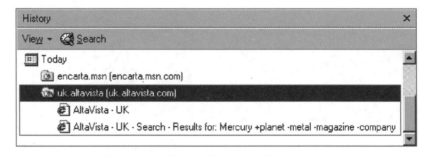

Figure 4.6: Expanding the History list

Tip:

If you click on any link, it returns you to that page

▶ Open some of the other days and see where you – or someone else – has been browsing lately.

As well as viewing the **History** list by day, you can also order it by **Site** or by **Most Visited**.

▶ Click the **View** button and choose **By Site**.

Robin's secret passion for flower arranging was discovered when the official website for "decorative pansies" showed up on the Most Visited menu!

Click here

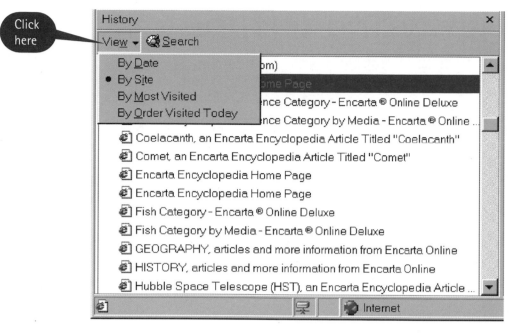

Figure 4.7: The History list ordered by site

If you can't find the site you're looking for, you can search.

 Click the **Search** button next to **View**, enter a name and click **Search Now**.

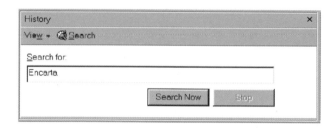

Figure 4.8: Searching for a site

This will list all the occurrences.

 To close the **History** list, click on **History** on the toolbar. ────

Click on **View** again when you've finished searching

Browsing Offline

When your browser is not connected to the Internet you will find that you can still see some pages you visited most recently. This is because **Internet Explorer** stores these pages on disk. They are only held for as long as the pages are kept in **History**.

Figure 4.9: The Title bar tells you that you are working offline

Internet Explorer tells you in the title bar if it's displaying a page offline. And you may also notice a news item looks rather old!

While offline, if you click on a link to a page that is not saved, you'll be prompted to connect again.

Figure 4.10: You will need to connect to go to a page that has not been saved

Refreshing a page

If you get a message that a Web page cannot be displayed, or you are not sure if you are looking at the latest version of the page, click the **Refresh** button.

If a page you are trying to look at is taking too long to open (the mouse pointer keeps showing an hour-glass), click the **Stop** button. This often happens if a page has a lot of pictures.

Selecting pages from the History list

Suppose you are doing a project on Ancient Egypt. You could look in the **History** list for the Ancient Egypt page you found in the last chapter.

 In the **History** window, click on **View** then **By Site**.

 Click on an **AltaVista** icon to show the pages visited.

Figure 4.11: Selecting a page from the History list

From here you can find a suitable site and open it.

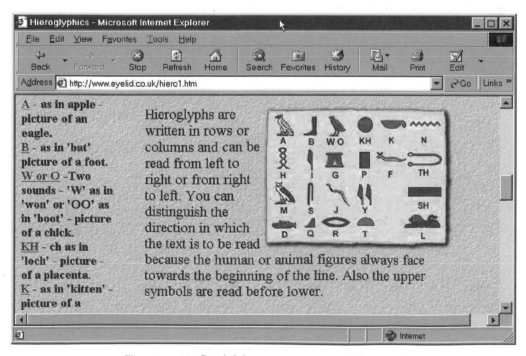

I've found a page on hieroglyphic writing but you may find something quite different

Figure 4.12: Revisiting a page in the History list

Copying text

Suppose you want to copy some of the text and graphics from this Web site into a **Word** document for your project. You have to copy the text and graphics separately.

 Make sure you have **Word** running and if you don't have a blank document open choose **File, New**.

 Go back to **Internet Explorer** (press **Alt-Tab**) or select it from the bar at the bottom of the screen.

You can select a few lines of text and copy them. If you want to copy a whole page of text, do it like this:

 In **Internet Explorer**, place the mouse pointer anywhere in the text and click the right button.

 On the popup menu, choose **Select All**.

This highlights all the text.

 From the **Edit** menu, choose **Copy**.

 Go back to Word and from the **Edit** menu, choose **Paste**.

You can drag the right indent to push the selected text over

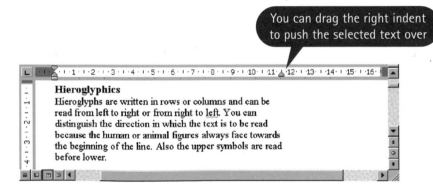

Hieroglyphics
Hieroglyphs are written in rows or columns and can be read from left to right or from right to left. You can distinguish the direction in which the text is to be read because the human or animal figures always face towards the beginning of the line. Also the upper symbols are read before lower.

Figure 4.13: Copying text

You now have text but you may not have any pictures, although Internet Explorer 6 copies a whole page as a table.

Copying graphics

▶ In **Internet Explorer**, right-click on the picture you want to copy and select **Copy**.

▶ Go back to the Word document, right-click on the document and select **Paste**.

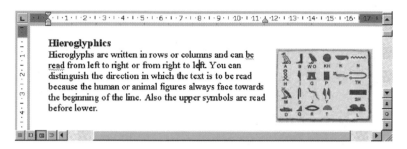

Figure 4.14: Copying graphics

Fee gets 10/10 for presentation!

Tip:

In **Word**, you'll need to set **Wrapping** or **Layout** to get the picture alongside. Right-click the picture and choose **Format Picture**

Note:

In Internet Explorer 6, the Image toolbar appears (usually) when you hover the mouse over an image. You can save, print or e-mail the image, or open the **My Pictures** folder

Chapter 5

Downloading Files

You can download pictures, video clips, sounds and software from the Internet. In this chapter you will learn how to find and save pictures and software.

You'll need to keep them in separate folders where they can easily be found again when you need them. If you don't know how to make a new folder, here's how.

Creating a new folder

 In **Windows Explorer** select the **My Documents** folder.

 Choose **File, New, Folder**.

Tip:
To open **Windows Explorer** click **Start, Programs, Accessories, Windows Explorer**

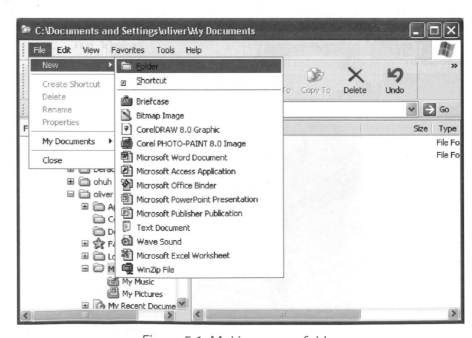

Figure 5.1: Making a new folder

A new folder appears in the right-hand pane.

Figure 5.2: Naming a new folder

 Type **Pictures** to rename it, then click away from it.

Looking for pictures

The Internet has lots of pictures you can download. Some are copyright but many are free. Let's find something brightly coloured, say a humming bird.

 Open **Internet Explorer** and connect to the Internet.

 Open the **Favorites** list and choose **AltaVista**. ———————————————————

 Click on the **Images** tab and set it for **Photos, Colour, Worldwide**.

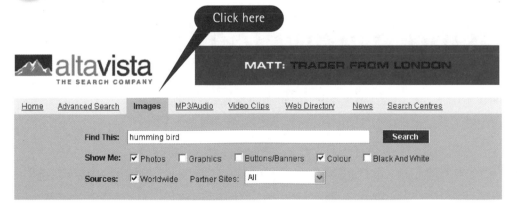

Figure 5.3: Searching for a picture of a humming bird

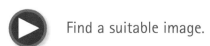 Enter **humming bird** and click **Search.**

AltaVista returns a few thousand images. Many of them are not free to copy – a popup message may warn you of this when you run the mouse pointer over an image.

Find a suitable image.

Tip:
To see how the download is going using a modem, hold the mouse pointer over the **Dial-Up** icon. A status message pops up

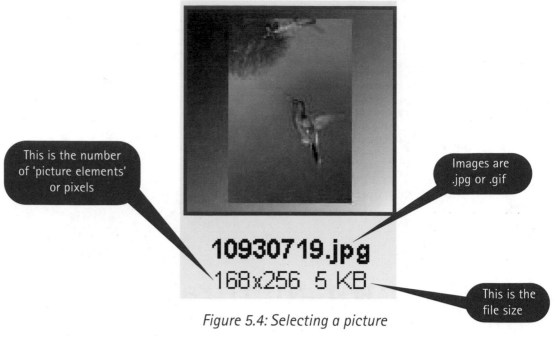

This is the number
of 'picture elements'
or pixels

Images are
.jpg or .gif

This is the
file size

Figure 5.4: Selecting a picture

▶ To copy the picture, right-click it and choose **Save Picture As**.

▶ Give the picture a name and save the file in the folder you created, or another suitable one.

▶ You can click the picture to see it at a larger size.

If you don't like these, check the next **Results** pages.

Using a downloaded graphic

You can now open the file in a graphics package, or put it in a **Word** document (using **Insert, Picture, From File**).

Picture files on web pages are usually stored in either **.jpg** or **.gif** format since these are compressed, giving small files which are quick to load.

Downloading software

There's a lot of software available on the Internet.

 In the **Address** box enter **www.tucows.com** and click **Go**.

This is the Tucows software store. You now choose a 'mirror site' for your region, like the one below.

Figure 5.5: The Tucows site

Click a tab to see the type of software you are interested in

Software is arranged by topic with lots of fun activities for art, maths, languages, music and other subjects. Programs are either for sale, shareware (you try before you buy), freeware or demonstrations (both free).

They have a review and a 'cow rating'– from 1 to 5!

When you click on a program, downloading starts. A dialogue may ask where you want it saved on your disk.

That's it for down-loading! If you're interested in sounds, you can find them on **AltaVista** and play them in **Windows Media Player** (or click the **Media** button on the toolbar)

Executable files

When you download a program file, it will have a name ending in **.exe** meaning it is an **executable** file. The program may install itself and start running automatically. Some **.exe** files are not the program file itself but a compressed or **zipped** version shrunk for faster downloading. The file is self-extracting. To expand or **unzip** it:

 Make a new folder as in Figure 5.1.

 Find the file you downloaded and double-click on it.

 Click **Browse** to find your folder, then **Unzip**. (If you got a black window, just close it.)

The original and much larger file will now be in the folder. If it too is a **.exe** file, double-click on it to install or run the program.

Tip:
Once **Acrobat Reader** is installed on your computer, you just double-click a **.pdf** file in **Windows Explorer** to open it

Reading .pdf files

Sometimes documents you download have names ending in .pdf – for **Portable Document Format**. To read them, you need a program called **Acrobat Reader**. If it's not on your machine you can download it free from **www.adobe.com**

Viruses

There is a risk that a file you download (or copy from a floppy disk) could be infected with a virus – a bit of computer code that can have various effects from mischief to damaging your computer. Make sure you have a Virus Checker program installed to catch the viruses as they arrive.

Hi honey I'm home!

Tip:
If you are on a network, it should already be protected

Chapter 6
Sending E-mail!

E-mail or electronic mail can be sent over the Internet to anybody who has an **e-mail address.** It arrives almost instantaneously anywhere in the world.

To use e-mail, you need both an e-mail address and a program to handle it. Both are available free.

E-mail addresses

E-mail addresses are quite like Web site addresses and made up in much the same way. The format is always:

username@domain_name

Here, **username** is you and **domain_name** is either the **Internet Service Provider (ISP)** who gives access to the Internet, or a Web site address.

Sam Brown's personal address might look like any of these:
sam_brown@compuserve.com
sam_brown@aol.com
sam@brownfamily.demon.co.uk

A school address would be something like:
student@hill_school.bristol.sch.uk

An e-mail address has no spaces and is usually all in small letters. It MUST be entered correctly or the message will come back undelivered. Every e-mail address is unique.

Some ISPs you may have heard of are AOL, Demon, Virgin, CompuServe, HotMail, FreeServe, LineOne, BTInternet, TescoNet, ... and more pop up all the time!

Tip:
Pronounce this as "sam underscore brown at AOL dot com"

Using Outlook Express

The program most often used to handle e-mail is **Microsoft Outlook Express** which comes with **Internet Explorer**.

▶ In Windows 98 or above click the **Outlook Express** icon near the **Start** button, otherwise select **Start, Programs, Outlook Express**

The **Outlook Express** window allows you to:

▶ compose messages

▶ send and receive messages

▶ reply to messages

▶ forward messages

▶ print messages

▶ keep contact names in an **Address** book

▶ file old messages in a folder.

Note:
This book uses Outlook Express versions 5 and 6 which look almost the same. Version 6 looks slightly different in Windows XP

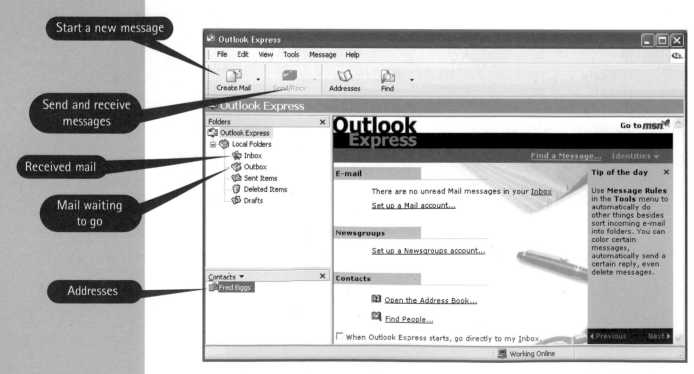

Figure 6.1: Preparing to send or receive e-mail using Outlook Express

Composing an e-mail

To start a new message to someone you obviously need to know their e-mail address.

 Click on the **Create Mail** button on the toolbar. ———

The **New Message** window opens.

New Mail in Outlook Express 5

 Type the address in the **To:** box.

 Leave the **Cc:** box blank. This is used if you want to send a copy of the message to someone else.

 Type something in the **Subject:** box to say what the message is about.

 Type the letter in the main window (the message box).

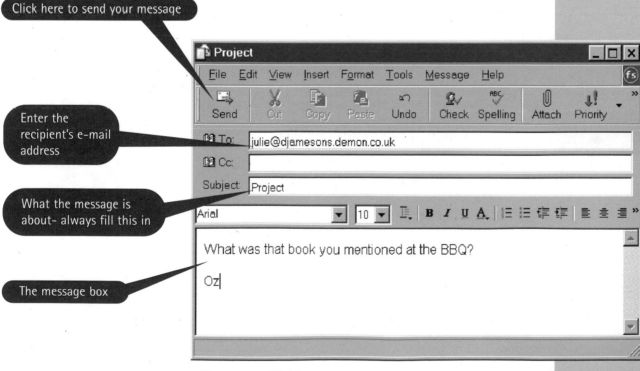

Figure 6.2: Writing a message

 Click the **Send** button on the toolbar.

 If prompted to **Connect**, click **Cancel**.

Tip:

Clicking **Send** is like putting a letter in an envelope ready for the post - it's not on its way yet!

The Outbox

The **New Message** window closes and your message is now in the **Outbox**. It has not actually been sent yet – you are still offline. You can write messages to several people and store them in the **Outbox**. When you are ready, you can send them all at once – this uses only a few seconds of online time and saves on the phone bill!

You can look at the contents of the **Outbox** and edit a message before you send it. You can also delete a message if you change your mind about sending it.

To edit a message in the **Outbox**:

▶ Click **Outbox** in the **Folders** pane to select it.

▶ Double-click the message header in the **Message List** pane.

Tip:
Having an **Outbox** means you can write any other messages and send them all at once

MESSAGE LIST PANE

FOLDERS PANE

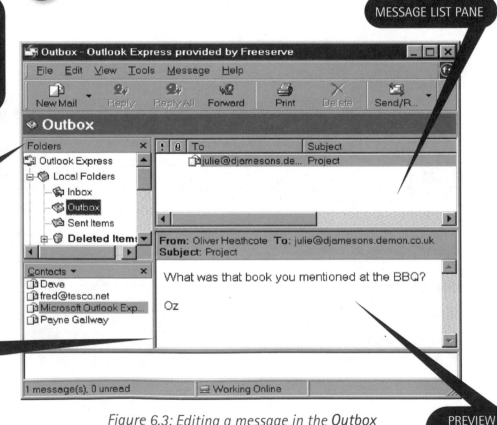

Drag the bars to adjust the pane sizes

Figure 6.3: Editing a message in the Outbox

PREVIEW PANE

▶ An **Edit** window appears and you can edit the message.

▶ Click **Send** to put it back in the **Outbox**.

▶ If prompted to **Connect**, click **Cancel**.

Sending a message from the Outbox

 Click the **Send/Recv** button on the toolbar. ————————

If you are offline, you will be prompted to go online. In this case click **Yes**, then **Connect** at the next prompt.

If the **Hang Up When Finished** box is checked, the Send and **Receive All** option disconnects you automatically as soon as all messages have been sent and any messages for you have been received.

Alternatively, you can send a message as soon as you have written it.

 Click the **Send** button.

 Click **Connect** when prompted.

The message will be sent straight away.

Tip:
Be sure you have disconnected after sending your messages, unless you have other work to do on the Internet. If the **Dial-up** icon is visible at the bottom right of your screen, right-click it and choose **Disconnect**

Robin's enthusiastic use of the internet had dire results for his Dad!

The Address Book

The **Address Book** is used to save the addresses of people you regularly send messages to, so that you don't have to type in their address each time you send a message.

▶ Click on the **Addresses** button (see Figure 6.1).

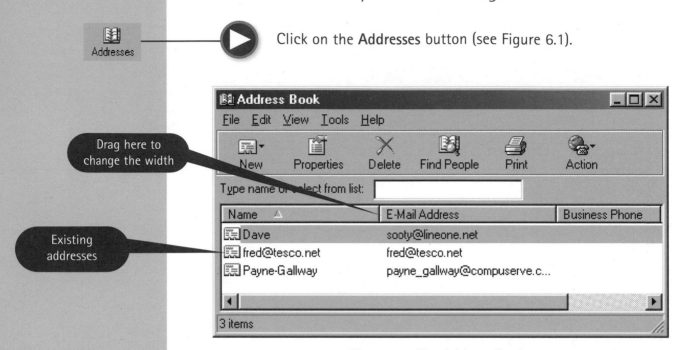

Figure 6.4: The Address Book

Entering a new address

The **Address Book** window lists any contacts who are already entered. To enter a new contact:

▶ Click on the **New** button on the toolbar and choose **New Contact** from the dropdown menu.

48

The **Properties** window stores the e-mail, home, and other details of each contact.

▶ On the **Name** tab, enter the **First:** and **Last:** names and **Title:**, with **Middle:** and **Nickname:** as well if you like.

▶ Click the arrow on the **Display:** box and choose how you want the name displayed.

▶ Enter an e-mail address.

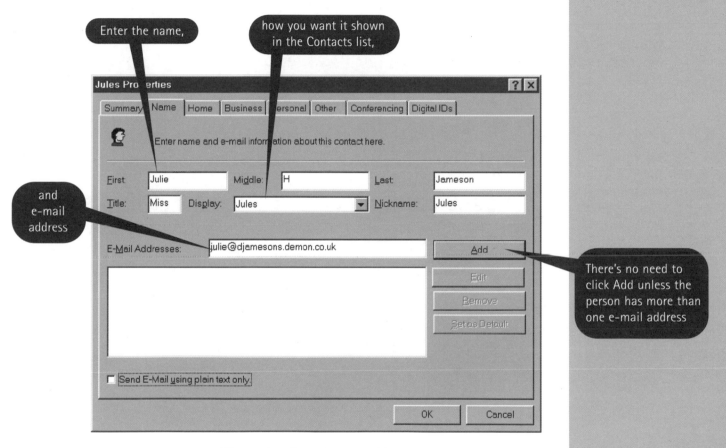

Figure 6.5: Entering an address

▶ Click **OK** to enter the address.

The name is now listed in the **Address Book** window.

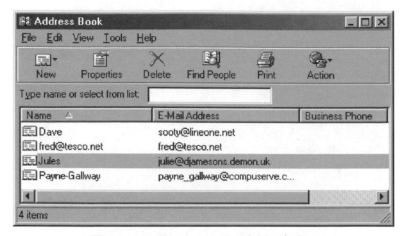

Figure 6.6: Entries in the Address Book

If you need to change it, say to add the home address:

▶ Select the name in the list and click the **Properties** button.

▶ On the **Home** tab, enter the details and click **OK**.

The **Properties** window lets you enter all sorts of details

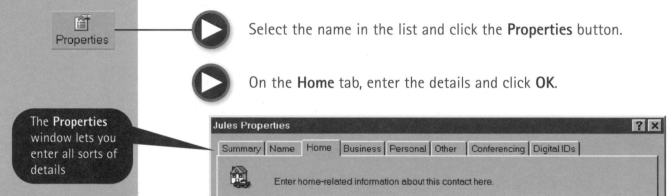

Figure 6.7: The Properties window

▶ Now enter two more addresses and close the address book.

Using the Address Book

You can now enter addresses straight from the address book when you send a message.

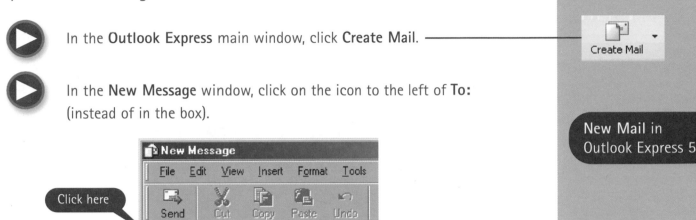

▶ In the **Outlook Express** main window, click **Create Mail**. ────

▶ In the **New Message** window, click on the icon to the left of **To:** (instead of in the box).

New Mail in Outlook Express 5

Click here

Figure 6.8: The New Message window

The **Select Recipients** window opens.

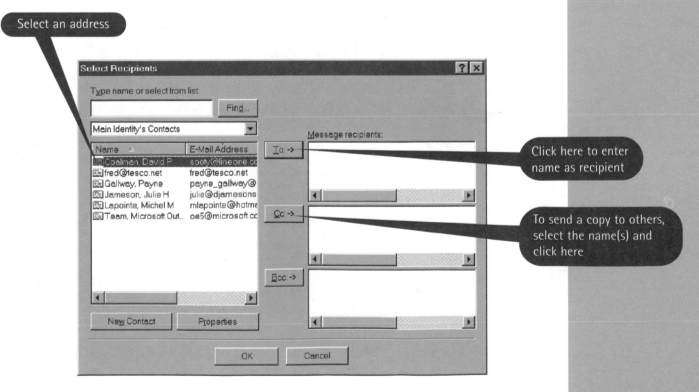

Select an address

Click here to enter name as recipient

To send a copy to others, select the name(s) and click here

Figure 6.9: Selecting an address

Selecting recipients

In the **Select Recipients** window:

 Select an entry in the **Name** list and click on **To: ->** to transfer it to the **Message Recipients** list.

In the same way you can send a copy of your message to someone else just to keep them posted.

 Select another entry in the **Name** list and click on **Cc: ->** to copy it over.

Note: Cc stands for **Carbon copy**. When the recipients read a message, they can all see who else got it too. To send someone a copy without the other recipients knowing, enter their name in the **Bcc: ->** box. (This stands for **Blind carbon copy**).

 Click on **OK** to return to the **New Message** window.

The recipients are all selected now.

Fee decided to invite all her friends over for a party - and all it took was one invite!

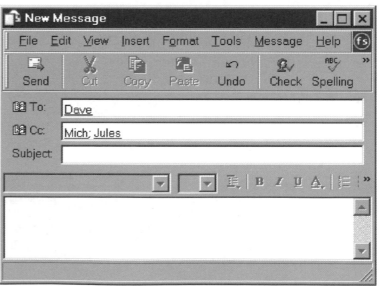

Figure 6.10: Ready to type the message

 Type in a subject line and a message.

Formatting a message

You can use the buttons on the **Formatting** toolbar to make text bold, underlined, etc. Notice the formatting options are grayed out until you click in the message area. As soon as you've entered the message you can try them out.

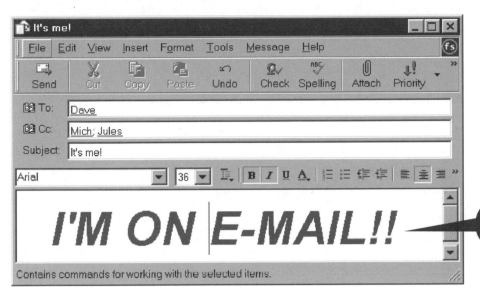

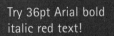
Try 36pt Arial bold italic red text!

Figure 6.11: A formatted message

Your message is now complete and ready to send.

Tip: Although you can format your message using **Outlook Express**, not all recipients will see the formatting. The above message received in **CompuServe**, for example, will look like this:

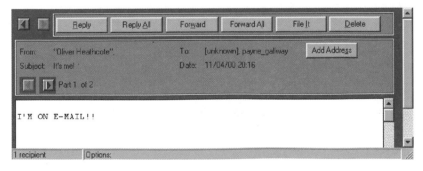

Figure 6.12: Formatting disappears in recipient's message

Chapter 7

Handling E-mail

Sending messages

As you have already seen, you can send a message straight from the **New Message** window but it's much better to send all the messages from the **Outbox** so that in case of trouble they are still there.

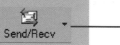

 Click the **Send/Recv** button on the toolbar.

If you are offline, you will be prompted to go online: in this case click **Yes**, then **Connect** at the next prompt.

Outlook Express now sends all messages from the **Outbox**, and if there are any messages waiting in your mailbox, it downloads them from the server (a computer belonging to your Internet Service Provider somewhere) to the **Inbox** (somewhere on your hard disk).

If anything goes wrong while sending, you could lose the message and have to type it all in again!

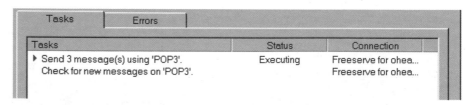

Figure 7.1: Outlook Express tells you what's happening

Recalling sent messages

Sometimes it is useful to be able to look up a message you sent last week or last month, to remind yourself what you said. All the messages you send are saved automatically and kept until you delete them.

 Click on **Sent Items** in the main window to see what you sent.

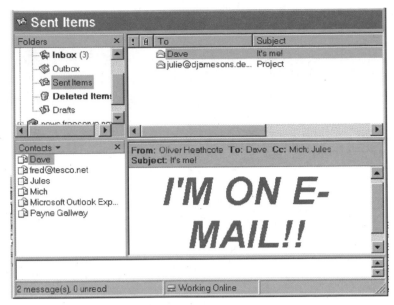

Figure 7.2: Reading a message that you sent earlier

Receiving messages

 Click on **Inbox** to show any messages received.

The number in blue shows how many
new (unread) messages you have

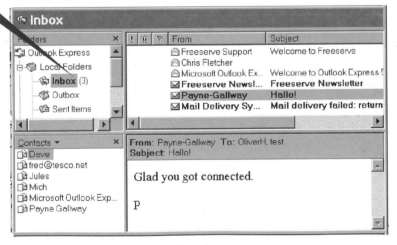

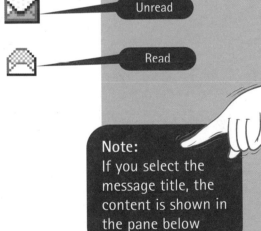

Figure 7.3: Receiving messages

Note:
If you select the
message title, the
content is shown in
the pane below

These are shown on the right with icons indicating **Read** or
Unread. The message is shown in the **Preview** pane below but it
is easier to view it in a separate window.

 Double-click on the message name in the **Message List** pane.

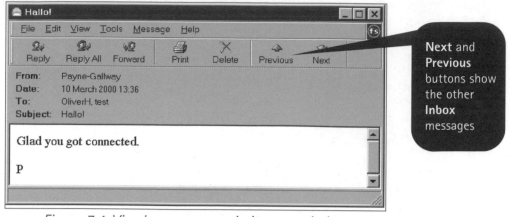

Figure 7.4: Viewing a message in its own window

In the **Message View** window you can:

▶ read and print out the message

▶ write a reply

▶ forward it to someone else.

▶ print a message by clicking the **Print** button.

Tip:

If you right-click on the name in this window, or on the message in the message list, you can add the sender to the Address Book

Replying to a message

▶ Click on the **Reply** button on the toolbar.

The reply window is all set up for you to type a reply.

The **To:** box is already filled in

So is the subject line

Type your message here

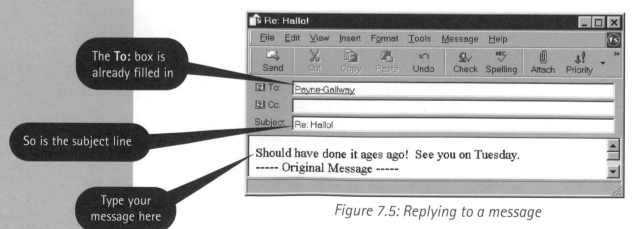

Figure 7.5: Replying to a message

▶ Type your message and click **Send**.

If you are online it will be sent, otherwise it is put in the **Outbox**.

Forwarding a message

A message sent to you might be of interest to someone else too. Try forwarding a message.

 Double-click on the message name in the **Inbox** to show the message view window.

 Click on the **Forward** button. ————————————————

Forward

The forwarding window is all set up, with a subject line of **Fw: [your message title]**. The cursor is in the message area with the forwarding message below.

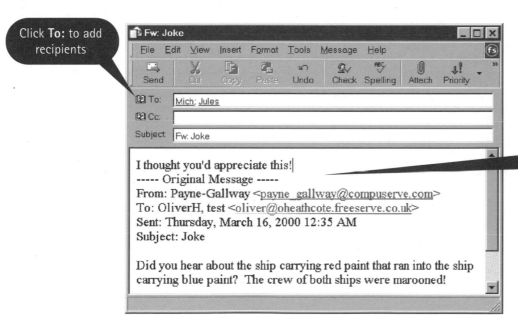 Click **To:** to add the recipient's name.

Click **To:** to add recipients

Add your own message here

Figure 7.6: Forwarding a message

 Add your own message if you like and click **Send**.

Instead of creating a new message and pasting it in, just **forward** it to the new address

Managing Messages

Once you have sent and received quite a few messages, they start to build up in the **InBox** and **Sent Items**. You need to **delete** those you don't need and **file** those you do. Rather than do this message by message, it's much quicker to select several at once in a list, and then either delete or file them.

You then have to scroll a long way to find a particular message

Selecting from a list

Suppose you want to select five messages in the **Inbox** list. If these are all together:

 Select the first, then hold down **Shift** and click on the last.

If the messages are not together:

 Select the first, then hold down **Ctrl** and click on each. Notice that this is a **toggle**: if you **Ctrl-click** on a selected message, it deselects it.

Deleting messages

It's best to be ruthless and delete any message you don't need to keep. This includes nearly everything in **Sent Items**. To delete messages:

Delete

 Select the messages in the **Sent Items** folder and click the **Delete** button.

Filing messages

You'll probably want to file some messages you have received and delete the others. To file messages:

 Select the messages in the main window.

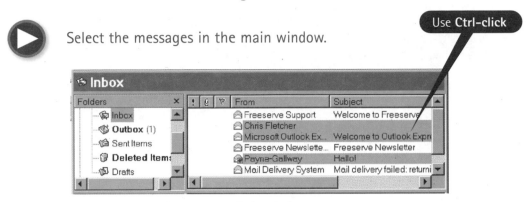

Figure 7.7: Selecting messages

Use **Ctrl-click**

Filing stores messages in a folder for easy identification later

 From the **Edit** menu, choose **Move to Folder**.

The **Move** window shows all the **Local Folders** you see in the Inbox. You need to make a new folder.

 Click the **New Folder** button and type a name for the folder, such as *Personal*.

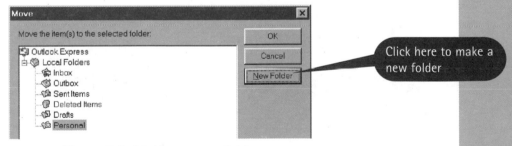

Click here to make a new folder

Figure 7.8: Making a new folder

 Click **OK**, then **OK** again to move the messages from the Inbox to your new folder.

Chapter 8

Attachments

This could be a word processed document, spreadsheet, graphics file, sound file, game file, etc.

As well as text you can also attach a file to the message. For example, you might want to send a scanned photograph of yourself or your family on holiday.

Sending an attachment

To attach a file in the **New Message** window:

▶ Click on the **Attach** button on the toolbar.

▶ In the **Insert Attachment** window, navigate to the file and click **Attach**.

This is the current folder

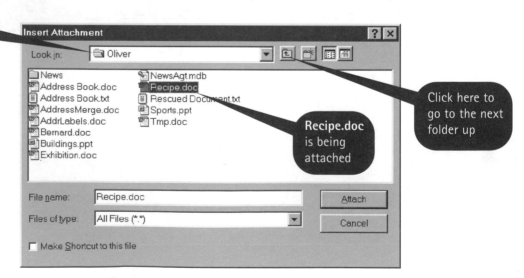

Recipe.doc is being attached

Click here to go to the next folder up

Figure 8.1: Attaching a file to a message

When you send the message, the attached files go too.

Receiving an attachment

If you receive a file with an attachment, the message header has a paperclip icon beside it.

Shows there's an attachment

Click here to see how many attachments. Note: A picture file may appear below the message

Figure 8.2: Receiving an attachment

Saving an attachment

You might want to save an attached file to your hard disk if you want to keep it permanently. Otherwise, when you delete the message you will delete the attachment too.

New	▶
Open	Ctrl+O
Save As...	
Save Attachments...	
Save as Stationery...	

 Choose **File, Save Attachments**.

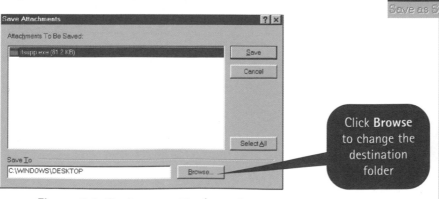

Click **Browse** to change the destination folder

Figure 8.3: Saving an attachment

The default folder for saving attachments is **Windows\Desktop** but you can change this with the **Browse** button.

 Click **Save**.

 Double-click the attached file's icon to open it.

Compressing (zipping) a file

If the total size of the file you are sending is more than half a megabyte (500Kb) then you should compress or **zip** it. It takes about 5 minutes to send 1Mb of data using a fast modem.

Most newer PC's have **WinZip** installed.

 Find the file that you want to zip in **Windows Explorer** and right-click on it.

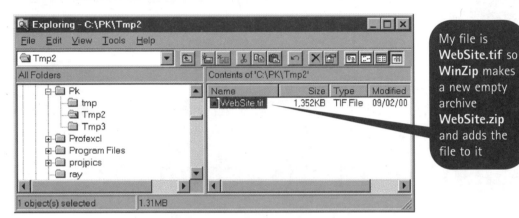

My file is **WebSite.tif** *so* **WinZip** *makes a new empty archive* **WebSite.zip** *and adds the file to it*

Figure 8.4: Zipping a file

 Choose **Add to Filename.zip** from the menu.

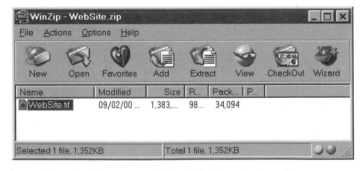

Figure 8.5: The WinZip window

The zip file appears in the same folder.

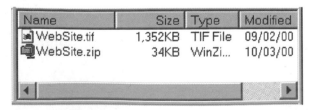

Figure 8.6: The zipped file is much smaller than the unzipped file

Sadly, this useful feature doesn't apply in real life!

Image files, as in this case, are reduced to a fraction of the size.

Unzipping a file

To unzip a zip file:

 Right-click on the **.zip** file in **Windows Explorer**.

 Choose **Extract to Folder**, and the unzipped file(s) will appear in a subfolder.

Self-extracting files

Although many people have **WinZip**, some do not and it is annoying to download a file you can't do anything with. It is better to make the zip file unzip itself and this is quite simple.

 Right-click on the **.zip** file in **Windows Explorer**.

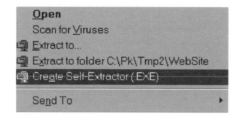

Figure 8.7: Creating a self-extracting zip file

 Choose **Create Self-Extractor (.EXE)** and click on **OK,** then **Close.** (You can test it first if you like.)

This process creates a file with the same name but ending in **.exe**. This is called an **executable** file: to run it, just double-click on it in **Windows Explorer**, browse to the target folder and click **Unzip**, and it will unzip itself into the folder.

Tip:
You can download it from
www.winzip.com

That's it folks ... you can now communicate with people from Alaska to Zimbabwe at the touch of a button!

Index